The Business Of Hypnosis

Cheryl Quinlan

DEDICATION

To the people I've met throughout my life who have taught me. To the people I know who have helped me. To the people I have yet to meet for the excitement of knowing new friendships await.

CONTENTS

1 THE BEGINNING

Have you ever been thrown into the deep end of a pool without knowing how to swim? That's kind of how I felt when I started in the hypnosis business. My instructors were all very good and the techniques I learned were solid but there was always something missing. Sort of a 'Now what? What do I do next?' I'm hoping, by writing this book, some of you will be helped by what I have been through to get started.

I have always had an interest in hypnotism. My earliest recollection was as a child watching television. I don't remember the show or who the female hypnotist was but

I do remember being fascinated while watching this woman in her large sparkly caftan knocking people out.

As the years passed, this fascination remained but moved to the back burner while my life took many different paths.

Around the same time I 'discovered' hypnosis, my mother enrolled me in accordion lessons that lasted throughout my school years. I was also involved in drama and music clubs. After high school I went to college as a music education major and began playing professional piano shortly thereafter.

Two times stand out during this early period. Our family went on a vacation driving across country. I decided to 'hypnotize' my brother by telling him to look into my eyes, waving my hands in his face like I'd seen done on television and telling him over and over 'you are getting sleepy, you are getting very sleepy.' After about five minutes of this, my dad stopped the car and yelled at me to cut it out because I was putting him to sleep. He actually had to get out and stretch his legs. A second incident happened in college. My two roommates and I were bored so I decided to 'hypnotize' one of them. It didn't take long before my 'you are getting sleepy, you are getting very sleepy' routine began working. Her arm became like a stiff rod of steel and the suggestion of 'at 10:00 you will start singing the Howdy Doody theme song' actually worked. And I was hooked.

When the opportunity presented itself to 'officially' get into hypnosis I took it.

I've never been one to do anything half way and have actually been accused of being anal about things. When I purchased a camera, I didn't just get a camera, I got the best camera and the best lenses, and the best batteries. When I started my DJ business, I didn't just get a cd player, I got the best cd player, the best computers, the best lights and lots of them, the best speakers, etc. I bought equipment I'll never use and never needed. This is only mentioned so you know where I'm coming from. Starting a career in hypnosis has been an exercise in restraint to say the least.

Having been an entrepreneur and CEO in several of my own businesses as well as Fortune 500 Companies, it has also been an exercise in laying the groundwork needed to make it successful. Unless the basics are done and done properly, the business will eventually fail. As I see it, there are two aspects involved; the business side and the Hypnosis side. **Hypnosis HAS to be treated like a business.**

2 DECISIONS, DECISIONS

Depending on the type of hypnosis that you choose i.e. clinical/consulting or stage or both will require a little different groundwork. As my background is in entertainment, I am focusing on stage hypnosis as a primary career with work as a consulting hypnotist secondary. With that in mind, I took a 'Safe on Stage' course put on by Justin James (www.thehypnosiscompany.com/safety) in conjunction with the National Association of Mobile Entertainers (NAME).

After passing the course, I purchased liability insurance through NAME. Insurance has been a much discussed topic through the years and people have their own opinions as to whether it's needed or not. My feeling is we live in a litigious society and people will sue for anything. The cost of the insurance is nothing when compared to a law-suit. Additionally, some venues may require insurance so it's best to have it.

One of the first things I did after that was to attend training. I am a firm believer in it. No matter how much you know, or how many years you have been doing hypnosis, leave yourself open for additional training. It's important. Firstly, you just might learn something and secondly, you'll meet some other people in the same industry. Way back in 1624, John Donne said 'No man is an island' and he was right. You can't do it by yourself. You need a network of people who understand when you say the back of room sales aren't great, or people you can turn to when you need support. What better way to have open dialogue than in a relaxed training environment. So, attend training-if not every year; then every other year.

There are many different trainings to choose from and it seems everyone has an opinion on them. Who offers the best training has been a subject of many heated debates in the chat rooms. I suggest you go where you get the most for your money. HypnoThoughts Live, geared toward the stage hypnotist, and the National Guild of Hypnotists (NGH), geared toward the clinical/consulting hypnotist, offer yearly conventions with a variety of training. Some hypnotists offer beginning courses and others advanced courses. Look around, take a couple of each, then pick the style you like and make it your own but get a good solid platform to build on.

State laws are continually changing and it is beneficial to check your states rules. Some states require Hypnotists to be certified by a credible organization or school. That being the case, I also took hypnosis training through the National Guild of Hypnotists (NGH) and received a certification as a Consulting Hypnotist. It's a good group, has standing in most of the states, and has been around for a while. Anyone can give you a piece of paper saying you are certified but is it backed by anything; will that person go to bat for you if you get hauled into court? Probably not so if you are going to get certified, be careful of who you get a certification from.

Then I took a stand-up comedy class at the local Improv. This helped me in writing material for my hypnosis shows and helped me learn to focus and get the point across without being too wordy. Additionally, it helped me to be 'fast on my feet'. Stage presence is utmost as is handling a microphone, both of which were reinforced through this training. You can see the final results at YouTube under Cheryl Q at the Improv. I would recommend this type of training for anyone getting into the business especially if you have never been on stage or performed in front of people before.

3 PAPERWORK

After deciding on the stage name of The Amazing Cheryl Q, I got what is called a domain name. This is the name used for a website. Some places to purchase a domain name are from Go Daddy or Webmasters. Then I built my website and submitted it to the search engines such as Google, Yahoo, AOL, Bing, etc.

Just prior to all of this, I registered the business name with the State and got a business/occupational license. (A lawyer or accountant can advise you whether to be a corporation or LLC. I am registered as a LLC.) You will need to check with your State and see what the business requirements are. Always remember, the way to be a Professional is to act like one.

I gathered up basic contracts from friends in the industry and talked to them about addendums/riders. This is an addition to a contract that contains specifications for travel requirements, green room mandates (a place where you can change or be by yourself prior to showtime), sound systems, stage and seating, and anything else that might be needed for a show. I then made my own contract. It was typed up with information I needed on it and is on file. Initial contracts should be reviewed by a lawyer to make sure you are protected. A sample of my contract and rider is included at the end of this book. Feel free to make changes to make it your own and remember to show it to your legal advisor.

Business cards were next on the list. They are fairly low

in cost so what I did was get two distinctly different cards; one focusing on the stage/entertainment part with the second focusing on the clinical/consulting side. Depending on who the audience is dictates which card they will get. Companies offering printing service are all over the internet. The company I used was Vistaprint.

4 SALES

Selling extra items such as self-help CD's, t-shirts, mugs, etc. either at events or on line is an added income source for many hypnotists. Self-help CD's for back of room and on-line sales were made early in my career. The resale rights were purchased as part of a training package offered by Dr. Jonathan Royle. These will be used until my own are recorded. Available are Weight Loss, Stop Smoking, Stress Reduction, and Confidence Building. If you are new to the industry and need something for back of room sales, contact me. Kunaki is a good place to get started with CDs/DVDs. They will send them out for you and send you the profits.

Digital downloads are popular and preferred with some clients and fairly easy. You put a link to the product on your website and the digital company does the rest. Gumroad.com, Sellfy.com, and Zaxaa.com are three companies that will handle the digital end for you for a fee. There are others listed on the internet. Be sure and check them out carefully before making your selection.

Some hypnotists make show DVD's for resale on site at the venue, also called back of room sales, while others take orders and send them out. Some provide a digital link for downloading the show. If you decide to do DVDs at the show, you'll need a good reproduction machine that can make multiple copies as well as DVD blanks, cases, and printing supplies. A good assistant or two is/are also needed. I use a "Produplicator copier" that makes five copies at a time. My DVD blanks and cases were purchased from Blankmedia.com.

I made T-shirts both for sales purposes as well as give-aways. Promotional pens with my name and contact information were also purchased. These were ordered through Discountmugs.com.

A good voice/video recorder has been obtained both for private sessions as well as stage work. If you are getting your own video recorder (you'll need one), make sure it is High Definition (HD) and make sure you purchase a video card that is 'fast' and long enough to record what you'll need. You'll also need a long lasting battery. B&H Photo is where I purchase my professional audio and video supplies from. The staff there is very helpful.

To professionalize the stage and sales area as well as for door advertising and excitement generating, I had banners/signs made up. A 5 ft. x 10 ft. was obtained for behind the chairs on stage and 3 ft. vinyl retractable banners for the stage sides/doors and sales areas were ordered. These were bought through Banners On The Cheap. The bases were purchased through Amazon.com.

One thing you will need to decide is what type of payment you will accept. Taking credit cards can facilitate sales but there are fees involved so it is up to you to accept them or not. When you explore credit card processing companies, take a look at recurring monthly charges and the percentage they take. I currently use Intuit and have the ability to process cards either on line or through a small card swiper added to my cell phone. PayPal is another option for taking payments. Their rates are reasonable and a business account can be easily set up. Of course there is always cash and checks, too. By the way, a bank account dedicated to your business is a necessity. **Do not co-mingle your business finances**

with your personal accounts. It tends to upset accountants and tax auditors.

Using social media such as Facebook and Twitter to promote your business is so very important. If you don't know how to use it and you can take a few classes in this area, it'd be beneficial.

Anytime you can get your name out there, do it. Look at various advertising sites such as Gigmasters for paid advertising. If you can get your name on sites for free, then do so. The more your name is on the internet, the more the web browsers will pick it up and will place you higher in the internet rankings. What this means is someone searching for you or for a hypnotist will find you faster because your name will appear on the first pages of their search.

5 MUSIC, SOUND AND INTROS

Once you plan out your show, you'll need to figure out not only your music and sound effects but how you are going to hear and play it. Venues or clients may or may not furnish a sound system. This should be part of your contract with them. If you furnish a sound system be sure and charge extra for it. Components typically found in a sound system are speakers, a mixer and a music source such as a computer, cd's, tablet, I-pod/pad, or smart phone and a microphone.

Speakers need an amplifier to push the sound out. There are two types of speakers. They are either powered, where the amplifier is built into the speaker which is plugged into electricity or non-powered, where the amplifier is stand-alone. The speaker hooks both into the amplifier and electricity. I prefer powered speakers. There are fewer cables to run, less equipment to purchase/set up, and a microphone or music source can be connected directly into it.

A mixer is an item where more than one music source and microphones can be plugged in. It adjusts the sound levels of each item individually so you have a good mix of sound. Mixers have channels which is simply how many items can be plugged into it. A five channel mixer will accommodate five items. Some mixers have an extra input for a microphone and/or cd players. Mixers are connected to the speakers. There are newer speakers that have three and five channel mixers built into the back of the speaker so your microphone and computer/I-pad/pod/smart phone connect directly.

If you don't want to mess with the sound, my advice is to hire a professional DJ in the city you will be working in and they will take care of it for you.

I've worked with hypnotists who use CD's and depend on the DJ to follow their cues (this is put in the addendum to their contract) while others load their show onto a computer and use a hand-held remote control to operate it. I bring both a CD and computer to a show and use a hand-held remote if I'm doing the show by myself. A couple of other hand-held wireless gadgets are; a hand held I-Jet remote that works with an I-Pad, I Phone or I-pod and hooks into a sound system; and a Bluetooth receiver that is paired and connected with the phone or device that contains your music and hooked into the mixer.

Don't forget a microphone. Wireless mics are great because there is no danger of anyone tripping over a cord. It is personal preference as to wearing a headset or lavaliere. I don't care for them as there are times I might want to speak with a volunteer privately. It's easier for me to just put the mic down instead of on-ing and offing a body pack. My friends at NLFXpro.com can help you with a good microphone selection as well as speakers and mixers.

When you are designing your show figure what music you will need and put it in order on your music devices with an outline on your 'prompter'. Please be professional and purchase your music. You will lose credibility and respect otherwise.

Royalty free induction music was purchased and will be

used for my own CD's (when they are recorded) as well as for the consulting sessions and stage shows. I will eventually have original background music and induction music available for sale so keep checking back.

Sometimes it's best not to leave anything to chance - you never know who or how your stage introductions will be made. At the suggestion of a former instructor, I hired a professional announcer to make my stage introduction. This has worked well and was worth the money. A promo video was then made and was posted on YouTube and put on my Facebook page. Fees for Announcements/Introductions vary and are usually by the length of the announcement or number of words. Professional voice over specialists can be found on line or another place is to check is through Fiverr.com.

.

6 SCRIPTS AND SKITS

Finding scripts for consulting sessions have proven interesting. Here again, the training package mentioned above from Dr. Jonathan Royle as well as the NGH training has helped immensely. It offered session ideas that I modified for my clients. Release forms for consulting hypnosis are mandatory. If the client is under-age or mentally incapacitated a guardian needs to sign them. Also needed is a worksheet the client fills out. This contains name, address, and other general information as well as a 'what ails them' section that will be used during the session. All of this has been researched, typed up and put in a special book that is taken with me for one-on-one sessions.

I encourage you to work in partnership and consultation with a client's medical professional as I do. Requiring a physician's approval for hypnosis sessions is a good idea.

Skits are mini shows within your show. A hot/cold routine is a skit, driving a car is a skit, etc., flies buzzing around is a skit. Skits are what direct the flow of your show. These usually start easy then get progressively more complex such as having dance contests or martians arguing near the end. Skits are individual. Whatever you can imagine can be turned into a skit for a show. Look at some of the hypnosis shows on YouTube. You will get a feel for what others are doing and how they are doing it and you will see a pattern of easy to complex routines/skits. Then develop your own show using your own style.

Some training offers the lay-out of a show and discusses skits/routines . The layout of a show or session is generally; 1) pre-talk (warm-up), 2) inductions (guiding volunteers into a hypnotic state), 3) skits or scripts as in the case of clinical/consulting clients, and 4) emergence (bringing volunteers out of hypnosis). When inquiring about training ask if developing a show routine and skits is included.

For stage shows, a useful item is a dry erase board which was a recommendation from Hypnotist and colleague Mike Valmar. I now have a couple of them that I list the skits on. They are put around the stage area as prompters to help keep me on track during the show. These can be easily packed and changed for the show's needs. Some Hypnotists use Tablets that are mounted on a stand or set on a table located near the stage area.

7 AND THEN

I always bring a 'mentalism' routine with me in case I ever get stuck and the show doesn't go right or just as an added something when I'm asked to perform longer. This is the anal me preparing for anything that may happen. I can also pull out one of my stand-up comedy routines thanks to the Improv training . You might consider having something as a backup for yourself. Doesn't need be elaborate or long but does need to be entertaining.

At some point you might want to set up a virtual office. It would surprise you as to the number of small businesses that subscribe to this. Having a virtual office will make you sound like you are much bigger business than you are and is more professional especially when you can have a receptionist of your choosing answering your phone and taking your messages. They will assign you an 800 number if you'd like or you can use your own number. There are several virtual offices to choose from all with different offerings and prices. I like Grasshopper.com.

I'm sure I've forgotten to mention something like having professional promo photographs taken and making sure you have a passport so I hope you will forgive me. Once you get rolling, though, remember to keep really good records for tax purposes. Consider speaking with an accountant early in your career and periodically thereafter so you know what you will need for taxes.

Never do a show without a signed contract. Make sure it protects you. If anything goes wrong it will be invaluable and will stand up in court. Keep it business even for friends or acquaintances. If you don't protect yourself, no one else will. Trust me you will be respected more for it and taken advantage of less. Don't ever sell yourself short – charge what you are worth.

There are a lot of decisions to make and lots to do to get started but if you do the groundwork you will be a huge success. Oh, before I forget, I recently found out the female hypnotist who so impacted me while I was growing up (and continues to do so) was the legendary Miss Pat Collins…..

Cheryl Q

Cheryl Quinlan

ADDENDUMS

1. SAMPLE CONTRACT
2. SAMPLE RIDER
3. HELPFUL WEBSITES
4. BUSINESS CHECKLIST

ADDENDUM 1 – CONTRACT SAMPLE

AGREEMENT FOR PROFESSIONAL ENTERTAINMENT SERVICES - BOOKING CONTRACT

_____(Client) hereby hires Cheryl Q Productions ("CQP") to provide professional entertainment services as per the following schedule of performances at the fee stated below and subject to the conditions of the attached rider.

Services:

Date(s) and Times (from/to) of Performance:

Name and Address of Venue:

Telephone number of venue:

Other:

1) In consideration for the services provided, Client agrees to pay CQP a fee of $_____. Upon a request from Client to stay longer, entertainer, at his/her discretion may perform overtime at the rate of $_____ per hour. Client agrees to a stair charge of $25 per flight which may be an additional fee added on event day.

A) Client agrees to pay a non-refundable booking fee of $_____.00 upon signing this Contract which must be completed and returned within 10 days from the contract date and will be credited toward the $_____ fee. The remaining balance of $_____ is due the evening services are rendered per agreed arrangements with client. Please make checks payable to Cheryl Q Productions. For Credit card payments fill out all the required information on next page and send back. Contracts may be faxed to 0000000000 (call first).

B) Cancellation: Should CQP's services not be needed on the booked date for any reason, CQP must be so advised in writing at least four weeks prior to the booked date or the Client is responsible for the entire contract amount. **Failure to pay the balance due 14 days prior to the start of the event (unless other arrangements have been made) relieves the CQP of any obligation to the Client but does not relieve the Client from paying the full amount owed.**

2) This Contract and attached rider constitutes the entire understanding between the parties, and there are no covenants, promises, representations, or warranties other than as set forth herein. No modification of its terms will be valid unless they are recorded in a written instrument signed by both parties. In the event any provision of this agreement is determined to be invalid or unenforceable, the remaining provisions will remain in full force and effect. This Contract will be interpreted according to the laws of the state of Florida in the applicable venue. In the event of breach of Contract, a court shall award attorney fees, court costs and related expenses to the prevailing party. **Any videos and photographs taken at the event by CQP and/or representatives may be utilized in future promotions.**

This Contract is entered into on the _____ day of _____, _____

_____   _____

Signed   Client:

                                              Street:

                                              Phone:

                                              Email:

ADDENDUM 2- CONTRACT RIDER

CONTRACT RIDER – TERMS AND CONDITIONS OF ENGAGEMENT

1) Client agrees to provide a covered shelter, heating, cooling and equipment protection from the elements to Entertainer during outdoor events. (If not available cover will be provided for a fee of $125.00)

2) Client will provide or insure the venue will provide a minimum of 10 chairs (or as many as space permits if greater than this) for Hypnosis performances. For the safety of volunteers, chairs will be sturdy banquet type and not plastic folding chairs. If needed, client will provide a sturdy 4-6 ft banquet table for use of entertainer.

3) Client is fully responsible to insure a minimum clear performance space of 10 ft x 15 ft. unless prior arrangements with the entertainer have been made in writing. Any stages with a height greater than 10 inches must have steps/stairs and safety rails on at least one side.

4) Client/venue will provide a grounded 15 amp electrical outlet to which no other equipment has been connected (dedicated circuit). In the case of the venue/client providing the sound system, it is agreed that it will have been fully tested and that there will be available for use by the entertainer two fully working electrical sockets and connections to run microphone and sound track devices through. Sound system must be located in a direct line of sight between the stage and location of the sound equipment and in proximity of the stage area in order to use the remote controls. If a DJ is provided, full coordination and cooperation is expected. Entertainer will provide a wireless microphone and sound tracks either by way of a labeled CD, computer, or MP3 device. If the supplied sound system is faulty, distorted or not loud enough, etc, it will be up to the entertainer as to the continuance of the performance. The full fee as shown is still due.

5) CQP will provide a sound system for an additional fee of
_____.

6) Client will arrange for a parking space for entertainer's vehicle and pay the cost thereof, if any.

7) Client designates _____ as the sole person(s) with authority to give directions to entertainer. CQP representative shall at all times reserve the right to control the manner and details of the performance of services as well as the ends to be accomplished.

8) Client agrees to provide non-alcoholic beverages, meals, and any other services to the same extent as provided for their guests for _____ people/person. In the event that no complimentary refreshments are being served to guests, the client shall provide non-alcoholic drinks or water as requested.

9) The venue/client will supply the entertainer with Hotel Accommodations on the evenings of
_____ which shall be
_____ double or king room(s) at a minimum of 4 star standard and shall include all meals, soft drinks/water and all expenses incurred. Client will provide transportation to and from venue.

10) Client agrees to insure the venue provides access to a secure changing room or green room for the entertainer's use before, during and after the performance. Green room shall have bottled water, ice, and apples for entertainer.

11) It is agreed that the entertainer may promote and/or sell their Hypnosis related products and merchandise, before and after the performance for a minimum period of one hour before and after the performance, retaining any and all profits from such sales.

12) It is understood by the client that all advertising materials and promotional items such as press releases, media advertisements, etc. distributed and/or displayed by the client/venue must bear the following legal statement and disclaimer as follows:
"Volunteers must be aged 18 or older and participate entirely at their own risk and free will, agree to be filmed and waiver any legal rights during this performance."

13) Client acknowledges the agreed performance will be copyright of the entertainer. Any recording of the performance, video or otherwise, can be allowed only with the entertainers written permission but is the

copyright of the entertainer unless agreed otherwise in writing. It is agreed that the entertainer may film any and all performances without prior notice, retaining copy, promotional and sales rights of said performance.

14) Client shall be responsible, if necessary, to apply for any license to perform that may be required and to pay for any fees incurred by doing such.

15) CQP/Entertainer agrees to have a valid liability insurance policy in effect at the time of the performance.

16) If the event is delayed as a result of entertainers late arrival due to the fault of the entertainer, Client has the option to either extend the show by double the time delay, or to reduce the fee on a pro rata basis according to the time lost. Except to the extent of compensation previously paid by Client under this Contract, CQP and/or representative is not responsible for an inability to perform due to accident, injury, illness, equipment failure, act of God or other condition beyond his/her control. Any cancellations will be reported to client as soon as possible.

17) If entertainer experiences an equipment breakdown and is not able to finish the show, the fee will be paid on a pro rata basis determined by the length of performance time. This will not apply in the case of damage to entertainer's equipment that is caused by persons or incidents at the event. CQP cannot be responsible for electrical problems or power failures, unless they are directly caused by CQP's actions. The Client will indemnify, defend, and hold CQP (and his employees, contractors, agents, and representatives) harmless from all actions, proceedings, claims, demands, liabilities, losses, judgments, damages, penalties, or expenses, of whatever kind, including interest, attorneys' fees, court costs, and other reasonable costs and charges resulting from the negligence or intentional misconduct of the Client or third parties involved with or present at the event, including guests and venue staff. To cover any such claims, the Client may wish to obtain a single event liability insurance policy.

18) Client agrees that in the unlikely event that the performance has to be curtailed or cancelled due to little or no co-operative audience participation then the full fee as defined is still payable. Entertainer has the right to cancel the show if the audience is less than 35 people and the full fee as shown is also still due.

19) Failure to comply with any clauses within this rider and/or the contract to which this relates may result in the show being cancelled and the full fee will still be payable unless otherwise pre-agreed in writing by other parties.

20) Any mistakes or objections to this contract should be brought to the attention of CQP immediately. This contract and rider should be signed and returned within 10 days after which it will be considered to have been accepted and all terms and conditions will apply.

21) Sections of this contract and/or rider not relevant to this particular booking are indicated by their relevant number
here:_____

_____

22) Any further clauses, conditions and/or additions to this contract and/rider are as follows and are deemed as accepted by signature and dating by all parties
involved_____

_____

_____

_____

Signed/Date

_____

Client Signed/Date

ADDENDUM 3 – HELPFUL WEBSITES

PAYMENTS
    INTUIT.COM

INSURANCE
    NAMEENTERTAINERS.COM

TRAINING
    HTLIVE.NET

TRAINING/CERTIFICATION
    NGH.NET

DOMAIN NAME
    GODADDY.COM
    WEBMASTERS.COM

CD/DVD DUPLICATING
    KUNAKI.COM

DIGITAL DOWNLOADS
    GUMROAD.COM
    ZAXAA.COM
    SELLFY.COM

VIRTUAL OFFICE
    GRASSHOPPER.COM

BUSINESS CARDS
    VISTAPRINT.COM

REMOTE
    BUYIJET.COM

CD/DVD/COVER BLANKS
    BLANKMEDIAPRINTING.COM

BANNERS/SIGNS
    BANNERSONTHECHEAP.COM

T-SHIRTS/PROMOTIONAL ITEMS
    DISCOUNTMUGS.COM

MICROPHONES/SPEAKERS/MIXERS
    NLFXPRO.COM

ANNOUINCEMENTS
    FIVERR.COM

RECORDERS/CAMERAS
    BHPHOTOVIDEO.COM

SAFE ON STAGE TRAINING
    THEHYPNOSISCOMPANY.COM/SAFETY

ADDENDUM 4 – BUSINESS CHECKLIST

1.   Stage or Clinical/Consulting

2.   State Laws

3.   Training

4.   Insurance

5.   Improv Class

6.   Stage Name/Domain Name Registration

7.   State Registration

8.   Incorporation

9.   Business/Occupational License

10.   Business Cards

11.   Contract

12.   Type of Payment Accepted

13.   Microphones

14.   Speakers

15.   Mixer

16.   Video/Voice Recorder

17.   Duplicator

18.   CD/DVD Blanks with Cases

19.   Professional Introduction

20.   T-Shirts

21.   Banners

22.   Professional Promo Photographs

23.   Music

24.   Sound Device and cables

25.   Remote

ABOUT THE AUTHOR

Cheryl Quinlan aka The Amazing Cheryl Q, has entertained thousands of people over the past thirty years both in the United States and abroad. Her interest in the art of Hypnosis spans several decades. She is an entrepreneur and CEO in several businesses as well as a management consultant for Fortune 500 Companies. The award winning Cheryl Q is a recording artist and has appeared in movies and on television. She is also a published author and popular speaker.

www.theamazingcherylq.com
www.cherylqproductions.com
Facebook: The Amazing Cheryl Q
Twitter: Stage Hypnotist@amazingcherylq